Broken Hearts and Rock and Roll

By Jon Blake

Series Editors: Steve Barlow and Steve Skidmore

Heinemann

Published by Heinemann Educational Publishers
Halley Court, Jordan Hill, Oxford OX2 8EJ
A division of Reed Educational and Professional Publishing Ltd

OXFORD MELBOURNE AUCKLAND
JOHANNESBURG BLANTYRE GABORONE
IBADAN PORTSMOUTH (NH) USA CHICAGO

First published 2002

06 05 04 03 02
10 9 8 7 6 5 4 3 2 1

ISBN 0 435 21453 5

Illustrations by Mike Perkins
Cover design by Shireen Nathoo Design
Designed and typeset by Artistix, Thame, Oxon
Printed and bound in Great Britain by Athenaeum Press Ltd

Tel: 01865 888058 www.heinemann.co.uk

628·6

Contents

CHAPTER 1

It is wise to pick your friends carefully. But if you want to be in a band, you can't be so choosy. I only know one person who can play guitar, one person who can write songs, and one person with a drum kit. It just so happens they are all idiots.

Right now I am visiting them, one by one, to tell them about our next rehearsal.

I start at Dave Smith's house. Dave's the guitarist. We call him Data, because he's half robot. Data knows everything about guitars and nothing about normal emotions.

The door opens. Data just stands there frowning. He doesn't say hello.

'What's up?' I ask.

'I've fitted my guitar with a new pick-up,' he growls. 'I told the guy in the shop I wanted it to sound like a Flying V. It sounds more like a dying cat! That guy must have seen me coming.'

'I shouldn't think so,' I reply. 'Otherwise he'd have closed the shop.'

I tell Data about the rehearsal and leave before he can tell me the rest of his problems.

The next stop is Cammo's. Cammo's full name is Cameron Crook. He is our drummer and a one-man disaster zone. He'd be a fairly good drummer if he had his mind on the job, but that hasn't happened yet.

Cammo answers the door in his pyjamas. It is 3pm.

'O.K. for the rehearsal, Cammo?' I ask.

'What rehearsal?' he replies.

'The band's rehearsal!'

'The band's still going, is it?' asks Cammo.

''Course it's still going!' I cry. 'Why shouldn't it be still going?'

'Sue said it had folded,' says Cammo.

'Sue? Who the hell's Sue?'

'Someone I met down the arcade,' says Cammo. 'Damn! That reminds me!'

'What?' I ask.

'Left me gran at the hairdressers!' says Cammo.

'Eh?' I go. 'You haven't got up yet!'

'Yesterday, I mean!' cries Cammo.

Anyway, on to Dirk, our singer and main songwriter. Dirk gets angry a lot. Most of all he gets angry because the world has not noticed him yet. Dirk, you see, is the greatest songwriter who ever lived. I know he is, because he tells me he is. Often.

Before I can say a word, Dirk is off on his own line of thought.

'I don't think we should get signed to a big label,' he says. 'Not straight away. I want individual attention. A small label is more likely to give me that.'

'Give *us* that,' I correct him.

'Yeah, yeah, us,' replies Dirk. He thinks for a moment. 'I wonder how much they're going to pay me?' he adds.

I don't bother to argue. Dirk may be a pain, but he can sing. We put up with him because he is our ticket to the Big Time.

Oh – there is one more person to mention. Gary Macey. Gary plays bass. He is probably the most talented member of the band, and certainly the best looking.

O.K., I admit it. Gary Macey is me. But I *am* quite good, except I sometimes wonder if I'm really rock and roll. You've got to live a bit to be rock and roll. You've got to get your heart broken in a thousand pieces.

You've also got to play gigs. Big gigs. Like the huge arena we're playing next week – St Jude's Church Hall.

CHAPTER 2

It is Sunday afternoon and I am in Data's shed. The end of Data's guitar is halfway up my nose. There is not a lot of room in Data's shed.

Cammo is late as usual. Dirk is also late, which is not so usual, and very annoying. Dirk has my bass guitar, which he borrowed to make a tape.

'What is this tape, anyway?' asks Data.

'Search me,' I reply.

Right on cue, the door crashes open. Dirk stands before us, his face like thunder. 'I swear, I'm going to kill that moron!' he snarls.

'What's up?' I enquire.

Dirk takes a deep breath. 'I'm on my bike, right, minding my own business. This car comes by and some *moron* leans out. 'Bo!' he shouts. So I go after them, don't I? I see they're stuck at the lights. Right, I think! I'll ride by and smash the bass against their window. See how they like it!'

'Smash my bass?' I gasp.

Dirk ignores me. 'I'm just about to get there and the lights change. The idiots get away! But I got their number: V401 VYT. A red Honda.'

'You're not using my bass to smash a bleeping car!' I say.

'No,' says Dirk. 'I'm going to use a bleeping sledgehammer.'

Dirk swings the bass at the cymbal, but I manage to grab it in time. Dirk looks round for other things to attack. Data gets ready to protect the family shed.

Twenty minutes gone, and music hasn't even come into it. Then, finally, Cammo arrives. He slumps behind his drum kit without a word.

'All right, Cammo?' I ask.

'Janie's dumped me,' he groans.

Disaster. Total, utter and complete disaster. Let me explain.

CHAPTER 3

No one understood what Janie Kemp saw in Cammo. Janie was the most wanted person in our year, and Cammo was the least. Janie dressed to kill, and Cammo dressed like roadkill.

But Cammo had a secret weapon. He just wasn't interested. That presented a challenge to Janie. And Janie was a girl who loved a challenge.

It took Janie six weeks to wear him down. She tried everything. She fluttered her eyelashes and flashed her navel ring. Cammo carried on dreaming and drumming. So Janie pretended to get interested in our band and they struck up a conversation. Janie invited Cammo to go babysitting with her. I don't know what happened that night, but Cammo went through the most amazing change. He took up a new religion, and that religion was called Janie Kemp. From then on, his days with her were numbered.

Now the axe has fallen, and it couldn't have happened at a worse time. Seven days before our big gig.

Cammo stares blankly at his kit. He has lost the power of movement.

'Just imagine the drums are Janie's new boyfriend,' I suggest.

Cammo stares in shock. 'What new boyfriend?' he snaps.

'If she had one, I mean,' I quickly reply.

Cammo rises. 'What do you know?' he blurts.

'It was a joke!' I reply.

He sits down slowly. He's not convinced.

'Can we get on with the practice now?' says Dirk.

Cammo slaves his way through the first number, though his mind is clearly elsewhere.

Then Dirk says he's written a new song.

'It's called "Till She Comes",' he says. 'It's about this guy getting stood up by his girlfriend.'

The door crashes. Cammo has walked out.

'What got to him?' asks Data.

'Data, he's just split with Janie,' I explain.

'Look, I wrote that song yesterday!' snarls Dirk. 'How was I to know he'd been dumped?'

I ditch the bass guitar and chase after Cammo.

'Cammo!' I yell. 'Don't take any notice of Dirk!'

'Just leave me alone,' grunts Cammo.

My mind races. I've got to say something –
anything.

'Janie hasn't really dumped you,' I blurt.

Cammo stops. 'What are you talking
about?' he says.

'She's testing you,' I say. 'If you beg her to
come back, she'll dump you for good. If you act
cool, she'll ask you out again.'

'Sure she will.'

'I swear she will, man! She's done it a
thousand times!'

Cammo's still not convinced. 'You sure
she's not seeing someone else?' he asks.

'Positive!' I reply. 'Listen. I'll put her on
the guest list for the gig. We'll play wicked, and
she'll be like putty in your hands.'

'You reckon?' asks Cammo.

'God's truth!' I swear.

Cammo thinks for a long, long while. I
quietly cross my fingers.

'Nice try, Gazza,' he says, and carries on
walking.

CHAPTER 4

There is only one solution. Someone has to persuade Janie to get back with Cammo. Someone like me.

Next day, after school, I follow her and her mates. When her mates go in the paper shop I make my move. Just at that moment, Dirk turns up. There is glee all over his face.

'Guess what?' he asks.

'You're growing another head,' I grunt.

'What have I been trying to do for the past month?' he asks.

'Get on my nerves,' I reply.

'Get us signed!' he cries.

I view Dirk doubtfully. 'A record company's interested in us?' I ask.

Dirk nods madly.

'Dirk,' I point out, 'we haven't even done a gig yet.'

'So?' says Dirk. 'They've heard the CD.'

'What CD?' I ask.

'The CD I've made!' replies Dirk.

'You've made a CD?' I ask.

'You knew I was making a CD!' replies Dirk.

'I knew you were recording something,'
I say.

'Well,' says Dirk. 'I had it put on CD. And
get this – it's been on *Radio Joy*! Straight up!
That's where these guys heard it.'

I try to take it in. 'This CD,' I say. 'It's not
the band. It's just you.'

Dirk shrugs. 'Same difference,' he replies.

'Don't know why you bother with us,' I say.

'I can't play live on my own,' replies Dirk.
'And if you don't play live, you can forget
about a record contract.'

'Well,' I say. 'That certainly lets us know
where we stand.'

'Yeah!' says Dirk. 'It does.'

I feel like hitting him, except he might hit me back. 'So they're coming to see us, are they?' I ask.

'That's right,' says Dirk. 'So you better get Cammo back before Thursday.'

'What?' I gasp. 'They're coming next week?'

'Why not?'

'We're not up to it, Dirk!'

Dirk stabs a finger towards me. 'You're negging me off, Macey,' he says. 'If we're not ready now, we never will be!'

Over Dirk's shoulder I spot Janie's friends coming out of the shop. My chance has gone.

CHAPTER 5

Next day I'm really prepared. I know where to wait and I know when to strike. I am like the cobra, except for the homework bag.

'All right?' I shout, catching up with Janie.

Janie looks round to see who I'm yelling at. She doesn't really know me that well, and she doesn't seem keen to change that.

'All right, Janie?' I ask, sitting down.

'What's it to you?' she says.

I laugh, as if she's made a really funny joke. Up close you can see her spots, and her sticky-out chin, and her badly-plucked eyebrows. She's not that beautiful. But she's got *it*, whatever *it* is. And *it* makes me talk like an idiot.

'You got a second?' I ask her.

Janie looks at her watch. 'I did have,' she says, 'but it's just gone.'

I laugh again. 'I need to talk to you about Cammo,' I say.

'What about him?' asks Janie.

'We can't get him to rehearse.'

'So?' she says.

'We've got this really important gig coming up, and…'

'…Are you wearing contacts?' she suddenly asks.

'No. Why?'

'Your eyes are normally that colour?' she says.

'Yeah.'

Janie squints hard into my face. 'They are contacts!' she says. 'They're tinted contacts!'

'Straight up, I'm not wearing contacts!'

'They're orange!' she blurts.

'So?'

Janie shakes her head. 'Freaky,' she mutters.

'Maybe I think your eyes are freaky,' I reply.

'I like things a bit freaky,' says Janie.

I'm starting to feel unsettled. 'As I was saying, we've got this gig coming up, and Cammo's head is all over the place. Can't you just be nice to him for a week?'

Janie stands up as a bus arrives. 'If you want to talk about this,' she says, 'I'll be at the Demons match tomorrow.'

With a little twisted smile, she turns and jumps on the bus.

CHAPTER 6

I have no interest in ice hockey and I am not (yet) a millionaire. For these reasons I have never bought a ticket for the Demons. However, Janie is their number one fan. She screams with delight at every crunching tackle. She shakes her arms at every goal like a windmill in a hurricane.

When it is over her face is flushed and alive. She grabs my arm and marches me to the nearest café. I have suddenly become her closest friend. She gives me action replays of every moment in the match.

'Can we talk about Cammo now?' I ask.

'Oh!' says Janie, her face falling. 'Him.'

'Just give him another chance. That's all I'm asking.'

'Boring,' says Janie, and drinks her coffee down in one.

I try to think of something to say against this, but nothing comes to mind. It isn't hard to see why she dumped him.

I pull out a ticket for our gig.

'Tell you what,' I suggest. 'Have a free ticket to our gig. Then at least I can tell Cammo you're coming.'

Janie takes the ticket. 'Can I have some for my mates?' she asks.

I give her six more. She pockets them. 'Ta,' she says.

'We're good,' I tell her.

'Yeah!' she replies. 'Good for a laugh.'

'You wait…'

'…Ooh, I'm no good at waiting,' she replies. With this, she lays her hand on mine. I begin to sweat.

'What's the matter?' she says.

'Your hand,' I reply, 'is on my hand.'

'Don't you like my hand?' she asks. 'Some people say my hands are my best feature.'

Janie lifts her hand to admire it. Mine suddenly feels very cold and rather alone.

'I wish I had your eyes,' says Janie.

'Then I wouldn't be able to see,' I reply.

Janie laughs. 'Witty as well!' she says. Her warm hand lands on mine again. This may seem pathetic, but I am now in love with her. She weighs me up with her jet-black eyes. 'See you Thursday then,' she says.

'What's Thursday?' I ask.

'Your gig, Dumbo!' she says.

'Oh yeah,' I reply.

'It's a date then,' she says.

'What does that mean?' I ask.

The little twisted smile is back on Janie's face. She picks up her coffee cup and makes to fling its contents at me. It's empty, but I still jump back. She laughs, gets up and waltzes away.

CHAPTER 7

Next day I call on Cammo. His mum answers the door. She tells me he's in his room and hands me a sausage sandwich.

'See if you can get him to eat this,' she says.

Hmm, I think to myself. This doesn't sound promising.

Cammo's room is a depressing place at the best of times, but today is the worst of times. His curtains are drawn, and the only light comes from three candles. Cammo lies face-down on the bed in a sea of dirty clothes.

As I move closer I realise what the candles are for. Cammo has made a little shrine to Janie, with two fuzzy photos, a birthday card, a hair clip and what looks like a toenail. Oh, and there's a handwritten note: CAN'T MAKE THE FILM TONIGHT – SOZ, J.

'What do you want?' he finally grunts.

'Janie's coming to the gig,' I tell him.

'How do you know?' he grunts.

'Sold her a ticket.'

Cammo lifts his head. 'Bringing her new boyfriend, is she?' he sneers.

'Cammo,' I say. 'She has not got a new boyfriend! Can't you get that into your skull?'

Cammo sits up and views me doubtfully. 'What's that in your hand?' he asks.

'Sausage sarnie,' I reply.

'Where d'you get that?'

'Your mum. It's for you.'

I offer the sarnie. Cammo takes it and looks it over, then sighs and puts it down on the bedside table.

'It's like she brought me to life,' says Cammo. 'And now I'm dead again.'

'Oh, come on!'

'Seriously, man. She put her hand on mine, and it was like being touched by God. Can you imagine what that felt like?'

A hot tingle comes to my ears. Am I going red?

'Cammo,' I say. 'You're not taking it in! Janie's coming to the gig! To see you!'

'Did she say it was to see me?' asks Cammo.

O.K. I've been honest so far, and it hasn't done me much good. Now it's time for a lie. A big fat one.

'She said that dumping you was the biggest mistake of her life.'

Cammo sits up, all alert, like a dog at the sight of a Bonio. 'Janie said that?' he asks.

'On my mother's life,' I reply.

'Then why hasn't she rung me?' he pleads.

'You know Janie. She's a drama queen. She wants to make a big romantic scene.'

'You reckon?'

'Picture it, Cammo. We play fantastic. The crowd's going ape. Janie flings her arms around you and begs you to go out with her again.'

'Yeah, begs on her knees!'

'And you say… "Maybe".'

'Or "yes"!'

'"Maybe" is better.'

Cammo nods. 'Yeah,' he says. 'That's what I'll say, "Maybe". When's the next rehearsal then, Gazza?'

CHAPTER 8

They come from all over town. They start in dribs and drabs, then merge to become a mighty flock. All of them have one thing in common – a love of music. Tonight, they are sure, they are in for the best night of their lives.

They are coming to City Stadium to watch U2.

Meanwhile, down the road at St Jude's, our first two customers have arrived.

The mood is tense – very tense. Cammo is worried, because Janie is coming. I am worried, because of what Janie might do. Dirk is worried, because FunBeat Records have not arrived. Data isn't worried, because he is Data.

St Jude's Church Hall is not very inspiring. But at least we have rehearsed – once. And Cammo hasn't lost it – yet.

'I'll just check the car park again,' says Dirk.

Dirk has checked the car park seven times now, but at least it keeps him out of harm's way.

'How you feeling?' I ask Cammo.

'Like I'm about to die,' says Cammo.

'We'll be fine!' I assure him.

'It's not the gig,' says Cammo. 'It's Janie. Are you sure she hasn't got another boyfriend?'

'Sure!' I reply, as that little warm buzz creeps up my neck again.

We sit back and let the butterflies flutter gently. A few more people arrive. Then Dirk suddenly bursts back into the hall, eyes wild.

'Car park! Now! All of you!' he gasps.

'What's up?' says Data.

'The red Honda!' gasps Dirk. 'It's there!'

'What red Honda?' I ask, baffled.

'The jerks that shouted at me on the bike!' says Dirk.

Data hesitates, but I get up. 'Come on, you lot,' I say. We follow Dirk out to the car park.

Sure enough, there is the red Honda he described: V401 VYT.

We watch as two guys get out. Dirk's hands curl into fists. The guys look up and Dirk struts towards them. We follow, trying to look hard.

'Nice car,' says Dirk, with a sneer.

'Thanks,' says the first guy. 'Is there a gig here tonight?'

'What's it to you?' asks Dirk.

'We're from FunBeat Records,' says the guy.

Dirk's fists magically uncurl. He shakes the man warmly by the hand. 'Pleased to meet you, mate,' he says.

Dirk spends the next half-hour shadowing the FunBeat men. He tells them all about our huge fan base in Japan, and how we turned down a contract with EMI. I wince. We've got to live up to this in a few minutes' time, and Cammo's reminding me there is still no sign of Janie.

'So she's coming, is she?' he grunts.

'I swear she is, Cammo!' I reply.

'She's got a new boyfriend. I know it.'

'Cammo, I've told you a thousand times.'

Cammo shakes his head. He's still shaking it as we take the stage. The band starts up like a sick outboard motor. Dirk goes crazy, waving his arms, trying to pump us up. But we are dying, horribly. 'Till She Comes' gets two hand-claps from the crowd. From then on it's all downhill. After the third disaster, we start arguing on stage. Data says he's doing one more song, then that's the end of the first set.

We start the last number. It's even weaker than the first three. But just as I'm on the edge of despair, something incredible happens. The song lifts off. Cammo has come to life.

Guess Who has walked into the hall.

My stomach flips completely. She looks fantastic – braided hair, glitter top, the works. I start dancing around on stage, striking rock-god poses. Look at me, Janie! Look at the boy with the orange eyes!

But what am I doing? What if she grabs me in the interval and Cammo freaks out? Should I hide in the bogs till it's time to start again? Whatever happens, we *must* get to the end of the gig. Our record contract depends on it.

The song finishes. Good applause. Dirk announces the interval. My legs turn to jelly as Janie approaches. Out of the corner of my eye, I see Cammo rising from the drums, flushed and sweaty.

'Hiya, Janie!' I say.

'Oh,' she says, coldly. 'Hi.'

Janie walks past *me*, breaks into a beautiful smile, and throws her arms round *Cammo*. 'That was wicked!' she says. 'Want to go out with me again?'

'Maybe,' says Cammo.

All energy drains from my body. All purpose disappears from my life. I pull the lead out of my bass, put it away and walk from the hall. Like a thousand rock-and-rollers before me, I am at last the proud owner of a broken heart.